THE IMPACT CODE

UNLOCKING RESILIENCE, PRODUCTIVITY & INFLUENCE

THEIMPACTCODE

The information in this book is based on the personal and professional experiences of Andrew Pain.

First Edition

Copyright 2014 Kissed Off Creations Ltd and Andrew Pain

Written by Andrew Pain

Book and cover design by Natalie Ballard for Kissed Off Publications

The right of Andrew Pain to be identified as the Author of this work has been asserted by him in accordance with the Copyright, Designs and Patents Act 1988.

Published by Kissed Off Publications

ISBN: 978-0-9928601-4-1

Copies for bookstores, libraries and public bodies available directly from the Publisher.

Kissed Off Publications

www.kissedoff.co.uk

CONTENTS

I always dreaded this time ... the day that Darren started his rounds.

I was short of my targets again and knew I couldn't meet them. I waited for his interrogation, rehearsing my response whilst steeling my nerves.

"What have you got for me today, Pain?"

Clinging to my best excuse, I complained that my sales leads were stuck in the pipeline. Of course, I was hoping he wouldn't remember that I'd tried this one the month before but with the sarcastic smirk I knew only too well, he too repeated what he'd said the month before:

"It's within your control. You have to believe. If you believe, it will happen."

He was full of it. He'd read the books and loved the spiel. In his world, if you screwed up, it was your fault entirely because results are bound to happen when you believe enough. It may sound outdated but Darren wasn't alone in thinking like this.

"You can be whoever you want to be."

"The world is your oyster."

"If you think you can, you can - if you think you can't, you can't."

Do any of these sound familiar?

Sure, each statement has its own grain of truth and your self-belief is of course an important factor in determining your success but in most situations, it's not the only influence on the outcome. Whether it's the U.S. President, an Olympic athlete, a successful businessman or woman, or a brilliant parent - each will have a strong level of self-belief which has sustained them through their respective highs and lows, but by no means as the sole contributor to their success in life.

If you're serious about making a lasting impact in your world, there are three essential personal qualities you need to master: 'Resilience', 'Productivity' and 'Influence'. Without them, your self-belief alone is unlikely to grant you the success you crave and it will be vulnerable when things go wrong.

Resilience - bouncing back quickly from your disappointments and mistakes, remaining wise and rational when you're under pressure. The more resilient you are, the more you'll believe in yourself - resilience and self-belief are closely linked and affect each other.

Productivity - pouring yourself into the important things, making big decisions wisely and promptly and delivering on the things you set out to do.

Influence - a persuasive skill which causes others to follow your lead - freely.

The purpose of this book is to deliver 24 unique insights which enable you to make the impact you were born to make. Each insight contains a blend of original and concise teaching, delivering accessible strategies to improve your resilience, your productivity and your influence ... enjoy!

BE RESILIENT

1) Resilient people see their problems as temporary and their strengths to overcome them as permanent.

The lights are on, the cameras are rolling and there's an eerie hush hanging over the packed stadium. This is your big moment. You've trained so hard, sacrificing time, energy and money but at last, the pistol fires with an ear-splitting crack and you're up and running.

Four hundred metres - one lap of the track - but you've gone off too fast. This wasn't in your race-plan and well before you're half-way round, you know you're in trouble.

The pressure mounts within you, you're panicking and you've lost your focus. In the final 100 metres, you've nothing more to give; the tank is empty and, one-by-one the other runners come past, all of them - you're last. You'd expected a medal of some sort, bronze at least, and the agony in your thighs is nothing compared with the crushing disappointment of the race ... just another moment in the life of an elite, professional athlete!

The ability to bounce back quickly from such defeat is vital for athletes who have basic bills to pay at one level whilst searching for glory on another level. So if we're talking about resilience, we can learn a lot from the big names of the sporting world.

How do they feel when they lose?

What do they say when they've been defeated?

Footballers, tennis players, cyclists: successful athletes and their coaches must learn to treat defeat as a temporary set-back, training themselves to talk about it in a way which supports this perception.

For example:

During the 2011-2012 football season, Newcastle United massively over-achieved with the resources at their disposal, finishing fifth in the premier league and playing some of the most exciting football on show that year. As a result, their coach, Alan Pardew, was rewarded with a 10-year contract, an amazing achievement in itself at a club where the chairman is renowned for his 'hire-and-fire' approach. During that season, on the occasions when Newcastle did lose, Pardew was psychologically brilliant in the post-match interviews.

"I'm really disappointed today on a number of issues"

(Alan Pardew, interviewed by the BBC on 3rd December 2011, following his team's 3-0 home defeat to Chelsea)

"We had a problem, today"

(Alan Pardew, interviewed by the BBC on 11th February 2012, following his team's 5-0 thrashing by Tottenham Hotspur)

Pardew deliberately emphasises the word "today" in order to embed the idea in his team that their problems are temporary. He knows that if he can encourage them to see things that way, the difficulties appear smaller (therefore more surmountable) and are likely to be quickly overcome. But if his players view the same problems as permanent issues, the situation can feel bleaker; discouragement then sets in, self-belief evaporates and the loss of points can multiply.

After the 3-0 loss to Chelsea, Pardew insisted:

"We never get opened up like that."

He uses the word "never" to convey the message to his team that his belief in them is permanent. Whether it's actually a true statement of his feelings or not, such use of positive language plays an essential part in strengthening the team's mental strength, which produces the resilience of spirit to sustain a successful team.

During the same season, Aston Villa Football Club didn't fare so well. Managed by Alex McLeish, they just about avoided relegation from the premier league and McLeish was subsequently sacked. It was widely reported that he'd lost his team's respect and it showed in their performances on the pitch. When Villa lost to Manchester City, McLeish's post-match interview shows an entirely different approach for handling defeat.

> *"To lose like that, we're unhappy and disappointed. If we lose goals like we did today, it doesn't matter if it's Manchester City or an amateur team, you'll still lose goals if you're not organised at set pieces."*

(Alex McLeish, interviewed at a press conference on 15 October 2011 following his team's 4-1 defeat by Manchester City)

Far from presenting the result as a temporary set-back or highlighting any permanent team strengths, he sows major seeds of doubt among his players by alluding to their performance as 'amateur'. As the interview unfolds, he then points an accusing finger at his team's poor defending, expressing annoyance that he'd done his bit in training leading up to the game, but his defenders screwed-up on the day.

> *"These things shouldn't have happened because we'd organised the players to be picking up the City targets who we'd singled out for attention. That's why I'm extremely disappointed."*

It's hardly surprising that McLeish's leadership style eroded his rapport with the team whilst Pardew's style inspired his players. Pardew has experienced some turbulent times at Newcastle United, but there's no doubt that his psychological skill (as evidenced through his language) was a major contributor to the team's achievements during 2011-1012.

Successful sports stars see their problems as temporary and their strengths as permanent ... and what is true for the world of sport can also be true for you. In order to bounce back quickly from defeat and ensure that your challenges do not overcome you:

1) Determine to treat your set-backs, defeats and disappointments as temporary. Deliberately use language that will help you to do that:

"I'm gutted at the moment."

"Right now, I'm really disappointed."

"I had a major problem today."

2) Accompany your talk of temporary disappointment with a statement about your permanent strength:

"I'm gutted at the moment because I know I can do much better."

"Right now, I'm feeling really disappointed that I didn't get the part I wanted because I know I'm a really good actress."

"I had a major problem today and if I face the same situation again, I'm sure I'll handle it differently because I'll be better prepared."

1) Resilient people see their problems as temporary and their strengths to overcome them as permanent.

2) Ignore unfair ... find the lights

Knowing she was stuck in a rotten situation and that there was no way out was agony for me as her dad. Whichever way I looked at it, I couldn't lift my daughter out of the problem she faced so I decided to sit down and talk with her. As we explored things, we agreed together that life can be brutally unfair; it always has been and always will be.

It may be an unfairness related to health which prevents people from living the life they long to live; or a business which folded in the recession and left them with a mountain of debt; or a husband who was loving and attentive until he became an angry alcoholic; or for many ambitious professionals, it's the promotion they thought was theirs, until they were overlooked by a colleague who they regard as weaker in terms of qualifications, experience and performance.

But whatever the situation and however unfair or dark it may seem to you, within the darkness there are lights which lift us. Amazingly, the more you look for the lights, the more you see them and the brighter they shine. But if you focus only on the darkness, the lights dim, some extinguish and eventually the day is lost in the night.

If you want to move on from your disappointments so you can make your desired impact in life ... **look for lights in the darkness**.

My daughter was able to identify some personal lights (her younger sister, her dog, her school) and she determined to recognise them for what they were: lights in her darkness. As time passed, although her unfair situation didn't change, she found more lights and they made a big difference to the way she was able to live through that time.

The ability to discover lights is as important for adults as it is for children and this includes both individual and team contexts. Irrespective of the job in question, when targets aren't met and the pressure mounts, morale easily sinks, something which only makes the predicament worse.

"It wasn't as tough as this two years ago."

"We're never going to get out of this."

"They just don't understand how much pressure we're under."

In such situations, finding the lights is vital to lifting the team spirit and consequently team performance.

For example:

I worked recently with the headteacher of a large school who'd been through a particularly tough time. The recent Ofsted inspection report had made grim reading; student absenteeism was high; staff morale was low and many of the staff resented the head and harked back to the 'good old days' of teaching.

When we discussed the possibility of looking for 'lights in the darkness', he was adamant that there were none to be found. In response, I asked him to describe his week's most frustrating incident.

He told me that the school boilers had blown and would be seriously expensive to repair as well as putting a key part of the building out of action. He added that on the same afternoon, staff had continued teaching even though it was officially too cold to work ... and there was his *light* staring him in the face!

It was a eureka moment for him: despite all that was going wrong, there were plenty of lights in the darkness, he just couldn't see them yet because he hadn't been looking for them. As soon as he saw his first one, he realised how many he'd missed, and the following day, he expressed his gratitude to his staff for their commitment even in such cold working conditions - which must also have been an unexpected but welcome light for them!

His school remains under pressure from Ofsted but he has begun the journey to establish a better rapport with his staff, something which will improve their morale and impact their performance where it matters most ... in the classroom.

2) Ignore unfair ... find the lights

3) Most of our problems in life are minor and temporary inconveniences.

There's always someone worse off than we are. From a global point of view, many of us are incredibly blessed but we allow ourselves to be incredibly stressed by mundane things like being stuck in traffic, not getting our own way at work, listening to our colleagues arguing and/or gossiping, feeling overwhelmed by deadlines or the list of chores at home ... and then there's the person who queue-jumped us at the supermarket and the irrepressible mobile phone we can't find and which we know we left on silent!

If we're always bogged down in our trivial frustrations, we'll struggle to make the impact we could in the things which really matter to us. Reminding ourselves that these are not 'terrible' or 'disastrous' events, helps us to maintain our perspective when tensions rise, something which relaxes us and keeps us in an optimum mental state. If most of our problems really are minor and temporary inconveniences, we need to treat them as such so we save our serious energy for the bigger challenges of life.

On a personal note, I find this phrase particularly helpful when I'm stuck in a traffic jam or being cut-up by another driver's road-hog behaviour (clearly, my driving is always impeccable!)

3) Most of our problems in life are minor and temporary inconveniences.

4) You only have one life but you do have plenty of chances. Don't regret the ones you missed; be ready for the ones you'll take.

We're told that cats have nine lives but sadly we humans have only one and the years seem to accelerate as our time passes. Before long, grey ('silvery') hairs replace our golden locks and life regrets easily set in:

"If only I'd done it earlier ...."

"If only I'd made more of myself when I had the chance ..."

"If only I'd taken a risk ..."

"If only I'd listened to my dad ..."

We all have them; broken relationships, failed dreams, missed opportunities, situations where we hung in too long or gave up too soon and crossroads where we simply took the wrong turn. Hindsight can be a wonderful thing but it can also be extremely painful.

For example:

Karen was a client I worked with, a successful professional but bitterly unhappy with her lot in life. Having been the bigger earner when her first daughter was born, she and her husband agreed that she would continue working while he became the house parent.

On the surface, it was a sensible decision but as time passed, her resentment festered. He was happy with the arrangement but Karen had always hoped to be the homemaker and her relationship with her husband deteriorated as she became increasingly jealous of his time at home with their daughter while she had to be at work.

As the years passed and their relationship became increasingly hostile, he focussed even more time on their daughter, which only served to exacerbate their problems. Now in her late 50s, she's paranoid that their grown-up daughter is closer to dad than to mum and bitter that she missed out on those precious early years. Rather than accept they both signed-up to the arrangement, bitterness has focussed her attention on her husband's low-earning capacity which she now attributes to his 'laziness'.

They're still together but Karen is plagued by one 'if only' after another and struggles with depression and alcohol. She believes she's blown her chances of the life she wanted and is stuck with the consequences of bad decisions made in the past, however well-intended they were at the time. It could be argued that she's in the wrong relationship and always has been but what's certain, is that she's still allowing herself to be destroyed by the bitterness of her regret, something which spoils her chances of making her most important impact - a top quality relationship with her daughter.

► Life is full of choices and we can't always know at the time whether the decisions we have taken are good or bad.

► We can't predict the future - we can't see in advance when serious tragedy will strike or when a wonderful opportunity will be offered.

► There are bound to be some things we love about our life and others about it which we dislike.

► Our expectations of what life should be like often clashes with reality. The problem isn't life, it's that our expectations are unrealistic or they're beyond what we can reasonably influence.

► Life offers all sorts of possibilities: they're always out there and they keep coming ... provided we remain open-minded, warm in spirit and as physically active as our bodies allow us to be.

It's time to stop dwelling on what you've missed or what still troubles you. Instead, set your sights on discovering an inner peace, which learns from your past and keeps your eyes on the opportunities in front of you. You really are never old enough for it to be too late to change your world!

Inspirational trivia: Colonel Harland Sanders was 65 before he achieved his huge business success as the founder of KFC - it really is never too late to make an impact and there are ALWAYS opportunities to be had.

4) You only have one life but you do have plenty of chances. Don't regret the ones you missed; be ready for the ones you'll take.

5) The only important question is: "How do we do it better next time?"

Recently, my daughter came home from school upset because she'd been given a low mark for an essay she'd just completed. Thankfully, she knows me well enough to know:

a) She won't be in trouble at home.

b) I'm not interested to know if the mark was fair or why her friend's shorter essay had received a better mark!

c) My main interest is to find out what went wrong so she can write a better essay next time.

Whether you finish second in a race on sports day or screw-up a sales pitch for a lucrative order; whether your team makes a mess of something you left them to do or you struggle to achieve a goal of your own, there's no point in thrashing around to pin the blame or sinking into self-pity. Apart from anything else, in the situations when other people are involved, as soon as you start finger-pointing, defenses go up; you learn nothing and relationships can get badly damaged. It can come as no surprise that people who have poor interpersonal relationships, rarely make their desired impact in life.

For yourself, your family, friends, colleagues: if you want to be your best, steer clear of the blame and/or self-pity culture. Instead, when things go wrong, explore one key question, the answers for which will help you fully realise your potential in life ...

5) The only important question is: "How do we do it better next time?"

6) If you want to conquer your worst, F5 rated fear, first conquer its F3 equivalent, because after that, the F5 fear won't seem so scary.

Don't you hate it when you're so scared that your knees knock, you're wobbly on your legs and you can feel your heart pumping against your chest?

It happens to all of us at times but if you want to achieve something significant, the chances are, that at some point, you'll have to confront some of your biggest fears. The other option of course, is to allow yourself to be ruled by your fears, but then you'll never know what you could have achieved and you'll certainly miss out on the abundant opportunities which were there for you to take.

If you summon the courage to face your fears, you'll find new possibilities opening to you and you'll develop your self-confidence along the way

There's a lot you can do to put yourself in a position where you can tackle your biggest fears. In fact, the small differences between 'those who do' and 'those who don't', is that 'those who do':

▶ Have well-rehearsed strategies in place to help them when they're feeling frightened.

▶ Are so motivated to get on in life that they're prepared to handle uncomfortable situations. They know this is part of the deal for success and they've come to terms with it.

I'll highlight some fear-busting strategies in a later insight but one of the best is to start by identifying a specific fear which you'd love to overcome. Then think of an equivalent fear which is not quite so scary and hit that one first. For example, imagine you want to conquer Everest, having never climbed a mountain before. You'll obviously try all sorts of lesser climbs on smaller summits before you go anywhere near the Himalayas. You wouldn't be stupid (or arrogant) enough to believe Everest could be your first mountain.

For example:

I recently coached Jack, a volunteer at a charity where I'd been working. Jack wanted to find paid work in administration but he'd never had a job, mostly because he was painfully shy. He'd hoped that the volunteering experience at our charity would develop his confidence, as well as improve his CV. Jack was perfectly capable with the basic tasks of work in an office: filing, data-inputting and other computer related work but he was adamant that he'd never be able to use the telephone.

I spoke with Jack and explained that unless we cracked his fear of the telephone, it would be unlikely that he'd secure a paid, administrative role. He agreed, (albeit reluctantly) and the coaching began. I asked him to identify his worst phone-related nightmare and he described a hypothetical situation of dealing with a difficult customer on the phone, with other people being in the office and in earshot of what he was saying. This was his top F5 fear and the very thought of it literally had him trembling. He was clear he'd never be able to handle it.

When I asked Jack to think of an F3 fear related to the phone, he said that role-playing a difficult telephone conversation with me in the privacy of my office would be frightening, but with time, he might be able to handle it. In the weeks that followed, we explored some negotiating techniques; we rehearsed different scenarios and within 4 weeks of our initial conversation, we were role-playing awkward telephone conversations in the privacy of my office. He'd overcome his F3 fear and would soon be ready to tackle his F5 fear.

Two weeks later, Jack started using the phones in the main office, taking all manner of calls (including the awkward ones) and with his colleagues working around him. Was he scared? He was definitely scared at first, but not as terrified as he might have once imagined and he now handles the office phones with ease. It was a huge step for Jack and a crucial point in helping him along the road to make his desired impact. I heard recently from Jack and he's just been accepted into his first administrative apprentice role.

6) If you want to conquer your worst, F5 rated fear, first conquer its F3 equivalent, because after that, the F5 fear won't seem so scary.

7) Laughter is like exercise: it's good for your health, you choose how often you do it, the more you do it the better you feel and when times are tough, it helps you cope.

My entire world had crashed. An acrimonious divorce and inevitable issues around contact with my daughters was bad enough, but the collapse of my thriving business at the same time left me with no alternative - to move back in with my parents ... at the tender age of 35!

Of course I was, and always will be, incredibly grateful for the support of my mum and dad but I felt a total failure and hit a downward spiral. In just two years, I'd gone from a highly successful business, owning two glorious properties in the South of France, two cars, a lifestyle of holidays and restaurants, to no viable income, no likely job prospect, one road-worthy car (only just), no properties and no savings.

There are a few things, which got me through those dark times: support from my parents, keeping a check on my alcohol intake, playing lots of football but, just as important, was the rediscovery of my sense of humour, something which helped me to re-invent myself and stay positive about my future.

The turning point came when I started to watch 'Mock the Week' on television, an irreverent round-up of the week's news by a bunch of highly talented comedians on BBC. It was a programme, which always had me in fits of laughter and I began to see that after watching 'Mock the Week', I always felt better about my life. True, nothing changed about my immediate situation whilst watching the programme but I was somehow lighter in spirit and more buoyant in outlook after watching it.

This moment of realisation prompted me to fill my life with as much humour as possible and I scoured the comedy scene for the comedians I most enjoyed from 'Mock the Week' (Andy Parsons & Hugh Dennis). It was slow but it was sure; my ability to laugh returned, together with a new resolve to rebuild my life.

Funnily enough, it was not long after that when I met a wonderful woman who later became my wife. I'd like to say it was a combination of my good looks and irresistible charm which grabbed her attention but, as she keeps reminding me, she agreed to a date because she thought I was a good laugh - I am so grateful to 'Mock the Week'!

Laughter is a wonderful gift which, like all precious gifts, deserves to be valued. When you laugh, you feel better about your life and other people will be drawn towards you if you're positive in spirit and at ease with yourself. So remember, when life is tough - seriously tough - your ability to smile, to laugh and to enjoy the mundane, will help you bounce back.

7) Laughter is like exercise: it's good for your health, you choose how often you do it, the more you do it the better you feel and when times are tough, it helps you cope.

8) If you want to be consistently happy, learn to delight in the things you'd normally take for granted.

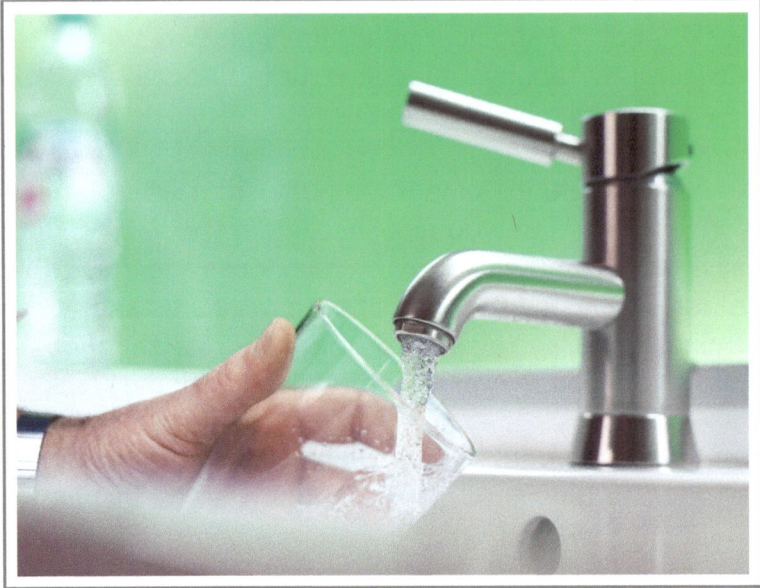

"I've had a terrible day."

"The traffic's a nightmare."

"You won't believe what he's forgotten this time."

So much frustration, so much going wrong, so little time to get things done and that's even before we've considered the travesty that Geoff next door (a smug joker at the best of times) seems to be completely unruffled by anything ... life isn't fair!

- ▶ Why's there always someone who's doing better than we are?

- ▶ Why do the people living at number 26 have the garden we'd love and the car we can't afford?

- ▶ Why are the couple across the road always smooching? It only serves to remind us of what we once had.

The irony is, that the people we envy are just as likely to be coveting something which we have but which we take for granted. However positive our outlook, it's easy to start looking at our world through gloomy spectacles, particularly if we compare ourselves with other people.

> *There will always be someone who appears to be better off than we are and if we become envious, the resentment and dissatisfaction soon follow - as night follows day.*

Real happiness comes from within. It's an inner contentment with who you are as much as with what you have. It comes from acting on your dreams whilst keeping a perspective on your life. So if you want to be resilient in the face of the highs and lows of life, then establish your criteria for being happy on solid ground:

A) Learn to focus on what you can do and make peace with what you can't: When other people are good at things which you're not, it allows them to contribute to your life and it frees you to make the most of your own gifts. And remember … some of the things you haven't achieved are easily explained by the fact that you were putting your energies elsewhere, most probably into something just as worthwhile.

B) Learn to delight in the little things: The running water in your house, the flowers in your garden (however small or untidy it is), the bus which turned up just when you needed it to and your elderly car which almost always starts first-time. Without a doubt, millions of people in the world would give their right arm to swap places with you - anytime.

C) Learn to be cautious when you compare yourself with other people:

Don't spend too much time on it.

Ensure you do it from a positive perspective.

Use the point of comparison as a means of encouragement in your own life.

Be grateful for what you learn.

8) If you want to be consistently happy, learn to delight in the things you'd normally take for granted.

9) No one chooses to endure life's harshest blows, but when we recover, we free ourselves from our trivial fears.

Which troubles you more often?

a) Your worst nightmare scenarios and the likelihood that they'll happen?

b) Your everyday issues which collectively may bother you, but on their own, are nowhere near as frightening as your nightmares?

If you're anything like me, you'll spend far more time bogged down in your everyday problems while your very worst fears lurk somewhere in the distance, bothering you only occasionally.

For example:

I used to worry about confrontation, hating it when people raised their voices, especially at me.

I used to worry about what people thought of me: Did they like me? Did they see me as a success or a failure? Did they regard me as 'cool' or as a nerd? (I simply wasn't the cool kid at school, which continued to bother me well into adult life)

I used to worry about public speaking, failing at something which mattered to me, losing my money, becoming ill, growing old, the mess I knew I'd make of any attempt at D.I.Y. - the list was endless and I was so caught up in my worries, that I allowed life to just happen to me. Inevitably, the good stuff was usually down to luck rather than judgement and as for understanding my purpose and inspirational goal setting, I had few clear goals at the time ... I was too busy worrying!

During 2008, I had no choice but to face-up to two catastrophic and personal events; the collapse of my once profitable business, (an enterprise which I'd always thought was secure) and the break up of my marriage, something which I knew would have a massive effect on my two young daughters as well as me. It was a turbulent time but I've come through it much stronger and more grounded than I was before.

I no longer worry about the more trivial things which used to bother me. Of course, I still prefer to be liked (don't we all?) but I've stopped stressing about what other people think of me, at least in terms of being a 'success' or a 'failure'. I'm more relaxed about money than I used to be, I thrive on confrontation and as for getting old, I'd like to be active at 85 but I'm deeply grateful for what I have today whilst being excited about building my tomorrow.

Because I'm no longer weighed down by my worries, I have the energy to focus on developing my goals and live a far more hopeful life. **If you want to make a bigger impact in your world, shift your focus from your worries to your goals and embrace the power of hope to fuel your action.**

My new-found ability to ditch my worries is a consequence of having to deal with things which truly terrified me. Sure, it's been hard but it's made me wiser and given me a positive outlook on the things that really matter. No-one chooses to go through hell but sometimes life deals us hammer blows which leave us no choice. When you're at your lowest points, remember … if you can retain a positive attitude in spite of what you face, you'll exit the bad times far stronger than you were before you entered them.

9) No one chooses to endure life's harshest blows, but when we recover, we free ourselves from our trivial fears.

10) The bravest people still get scared but meet their fears with well-rehearsed strategies.

There's a similarity between brave people and scaredy cats ... and a big difference too.

Like scaredy cats, brave people know what it is to feel fear and still experience the symptoms of a pounding chest, feeling sick and shaky knees, but the similarities end there. Not only do brave people refuse to surrender to their fears, they deliberately put themselves into situations which they know will scare them and they understand that making a lasting impact depends on overcoming many of their fears. Because they recognise this as part of the deal for success, they sensibly develop strategies to help them through the scary times.

By contrast, scaredy cats will do anything to give fear a miss. After all, who actually wants to be afraid when you could be comfortable? Consequently, scaredy cats restrict both their opportunities and their potential impact, and they become so anxious about being frightened, that their purpose in life is to avoid scary situations. Consequently, they no longer live life to the full - a much more worrying way to live!

In order to move from 'timidity' to 'courage':

Step 1) Take a conscious decision to attempt some things, which you'd usually be too scared/worried to consider.

Step 2) Develop strategies that will make a difference when you're afraid. If you want to overcome your fears, your success in the heat of the moment will come down to the effectiveness of your strategies and your ability to use them. If you don't have any strategies, your determination alone may not be enough to carry you through.

For example:

I was never great with heights but my natural reluctance became an all-consuming fear when I spent a year working in Mexico. Towards the end of my time there, I visited a number of ancient Mayan temples and braved the horrifically steep stairs to the top. It may sound a bit lame but the signs at the bottom which remind tourists that they're climbing at their own risk are there for a reason (if you've never been to Mexico, check out Uxmal on Google images and you'll see what I mean).

Later, after my two daughters were born, I decided to conquer my phobia of heights as I didn't want to be forever avoiding doing cool stuff with them. So, I began with a few days at the local aerial assault course set high in the trees and used three strategies to give me a chance of finishing what I'd started:

1) Gratitude: When you're feeling the fear, search your mind for the things about that situation, which make you feel truly thankful.

At one point, I was suspended 15 metres up in the trees (harnessed of course). Before I started to inch my way across the wire rope, I consciously thanked the world for the wonder of what was around me: a beautiful woodland and a glorious sunny day. I was deliberately mindful of my conspicuous good health which enabled me to try the assault course in the first place and was grateful for the pair of quality trainers on my feet which were proving their worth on the course. Gratitude is an effective calming tonic, it's up to you to use it to its fullest.

2) What's the worst that can happen? Back in the 1920s, renowned thinker, Dale Carnegie, had some great things to say about 'worry'. He suggested:

a) Identify the worst thing about the worrying situation that could happen.

b) Decide whether or not you can deal with it.

c) If you could deal with it: remind yourself that you can deal with the worst and take action to prevent it from happening.

This is powerful stuff and I would go further: when you're clear about the worst thing that could happen, if you don't think you could actually deal with it, look again. If you're still convinced that it's too much for you, ask yourself what you have to do in order to get to the place where you could deal with it one day and take action to start equipping yourself.

Suspended up in the trees, I decided that the worst that could happen would be to fall and die or break my neck. Could I handle that? Well, it's not my top choice for sure (I reasoned) but it will only happen if I don't fix my harnesses properly. And so, at each junction on the assault course, I double-checked the harness to be sure everything was in place. So, knowing my harnesses were ok, the worst that could now happen was that I'd slip and hang in mid-air, held by my harness. Unnerving? Very, but that's all. Could I deal with that? Possibly I guess - it wouldn't break my neck and I'd obviously live. So, I'll do what I can to avoid a fall or a slip but it's no longer a 'doom & gloom' issue.

3) Identify which of your unique qualities will help you achieve your goal:

It makes sense to examine what could go wrong when you're building up to a major performance or test. But once show-time comes and you're ON, you're more likely to screw-up if you're still tormenting yourself with the things which could go wrong.

When the **NOW** time has come: think positively about your own achievements; your gifts and your qualities and be clear about how they'll help you deliver the impact you want to make. While I was on the assault course, battling with fear, I told myself that as a (fairly) fit man in his prime (I was 33 at the time), I had to be well placed physically to handle any challenge this course could throw at me. As for the mental struggle, I'd faced some particularly tough things in the months before attempting the course and the strength I'd shown in getting through them would now stand me in good stead.

It may be an exam, or a penalty shoot-out to decide the outcome of the World Cup; a vital business pitch, or an awkward situation at home, but when show-time comes, focus on your proven qualities and determine that they'll be the decisive factor for a positive outcome.

10) The bravest people still get scared but meet their fears with well-rehearsed strategies.

BE PRODUCTIVE

11) Productive people know when to save their energy and when to invest it.

Like Winston Churchill, I used to be a firm believer in the mantra 'never ever give up' until I realised that my natural tenacity caused me untold stress and wasted time by keeping me hanging on to lost causes.

For example:

Elaine is desperate for her husband, John, to change. Sadly, after prolonged marriage counselling and endless drunken rows, it's clear that John won't get to grips with his drink problem, certainly not in the foreseeable future.

Never give up? Really?

Jane is in her late 20s and has given up everything to pursue a career in acting. She excels at drama but her sacrifices have come to nothing. She's saddled with debts she can't pay and is utterly crushed by a continuing succession of one rejection after another ...

Never give up? Really?

What about ... **"WAKE UP AND SMELL THE COFFEE!"**

Most of us would agree that persistence is a vital contributor to success in life but so is sound judgement. If you want to make a bigger impact in your world, then productivity is key to making things happen, but there are only seven days in a week and you only have so much energy to invest so it's vital you're wise in how you invest it.

My advance of 'never ever give up' follows years of mixed fortunes and probably draws on the world of mountaineering. It comes in three distinct parts and helps me to accompany my natural tenacity with practiced wisdom.

▶ Change course when it's wise to do so.

The best mountaineers stop climbing if their health or the weather conditions deteriorate. They pause to assess the situation and examine whether their attempt on the summit is beyond their ability at this time. Plenty would turn back, disappointed, but conscious of a wise decision made. Only a few would keep going in such circumstances and possibly with tragic conclusions.

▶ Always move forward ... avoid going round in circles.

The best mountaineers know that energy and time have limitations. Therefore, they'll either move forward, or in certain circumstances and if the logic supports it, they may turn back, but they'll never knowingly go round in circles and will plan their route carefully to avoid doing so.

▶ When you look back, celebrate the progression you've made - don't fuss over the paths you could have taken.

Everyone looks back from time to time and having done a few moderate climbs in my life, I know that the higher you climb, the more exhilarating the view and satisfying the progress. So when you're scanning the horizon with the wind in your hair, what's the point in dwelling on whether you could have climbed a different mountain or whether it might have been better to stay at base camp for longer? Enjoy the view, be grateful for what you've learned and keep going!

If we're serious about making our mark where it matters most, we need to be selective about where we invest our energy so we don't waste our efforts on pursuits which either lead us nowhere or take us off course. Learn to:

▶ Target situations where you can make a positive impact.

▶ Withdraw from the things which damage you.

▶ Alter your approach when it's wise to do so.

▶ 'Park' the things which could work well in the future but for which 'now' is not the right time.

Invest wisely by focussing on your most important goals. Remember that regret, worry and wishful thinking (dreaming about things which you can't influence or which you have no intention of taking action on) will always offer a poor return on your investment of time.

11) Productive people know when to save their energy and when to invest it.

12) Wise generals pick their battles and live long lives; brave warriors fight all their battles and die young.

Too many of us limit our impact in life because of a common habit ... we jump into battles which we simply can't win.

Some of us launch our assault at the wrong time; some are totally unprepared for what lies ahead; others impulsively wade in, even when the odds are clearly stacked against them.

Our world is fast-moving and unsurprisingly, we face a variety of battles throughout our lives. If we try to fight most of them; we become exhausted from the warfare, we get frustrated by the results, (which often don't go our way) and ultimately, we make catastrophic errors of judgement when the battles commence - it's a vicious circle. But when we learn to pick our 'fights' and concentrate our resources on the important ones and the ones we can win, we avoid the futile disputes, saving our precious mental and physical energy for the situations where we can really make our desired impact.

For example:

You're determined to make your board members see sense. Their refusal to move in what you believe to be the right direction is incredibly frustrating, leaving you to conclude that their caution owes far more to stubbornness than competence.

You 'know' you're right and it's tempting to press your agenda because you've decided that you're the only one with any real sense of the bigger picture. But if the board absolutely refuses to budge, you'll need to watch that you don't end up going round in angry circles of dispute which damage your work relationships to such an extent, that what began as a disagreement on direction, sinks into an all-out war of attrition. There are times when (whoever we are and whoever they are):

We can't change other people.

We can't influence everyone.

We need to accept what we can't change.

We'll be happier (and a lot more productive) if we channel our energies into the things we can change.

On the occasions where you're clear that it's time to confront or challenge, make sure you've established some firm personal boundaries which guide your decision making and ensure that your actions are reasoned and logical.

I. Focus on important battles. Don't respond to every issue. Wise generals value peace and understand that even the best troops need a time of rest and reflection. Whenever hostilities loom on your horizon, ask yourself:

Is this really worth it?

Am I about to go to war for a positive long-term outcome or merely to get my own way and prove I'm right?

To what extent is my ego controlling my actions?

Do I actually have the resources for this fight?

II. Ensure you choose the right time to go to battle. Any military leader would tell you that victory is not simply down to tactics, military resources and superior weapons; 'timing' can be critical in determining the outcome. Sometimes it really is best to leave well alone whilst keeping half an eye on the situation. Ask yourself:

What's the best and worst that can happen if I hold back instead of pitching in?

If I leave alone for now and revisit the issue in a week's time, could things look different to how I see them right now?

III. Fight the battles you can win. Why waste your energy on something you know you'll lose? Sure, occasionally, situations will arise where you know you're going to lose but you believe it's a matter of integrity to put up a fight. But, ask yourself:

What will I gain from going to war? (If your answer is ... "I'll feel better about it", I suggest you think again!)

What are the consequences for me of losing? Can I handle them and is it worth it?

IV. Avoid an aggressive approach. In the majority of life situations, going into battle is a very different matter from a literal military confrontation and for one particular reason: in a normal life context, the less aggressive you are from the beginning, the more likely it is that you'll end up with what you want.

When we're on the receiving end of aggression, we tend to become defensive (or equally aggressive), which means that the barriers go up and we aren't listening anymore. As a result, when arguments begin aggressively, they become drawn out, no-one makes headway, everyone wastes time and any apparent victory is sufficiently resented that ongoing relationships will be under constant threat.

The more peaceful your approach, the more likely you'll generate a mutually satisfactory outcome which is the only guarantee of long lasting peace. Your time is precious; your energy is precious; neither is limitless.

12) Wise generals pick their battles and live long lives; brave warriors fight all their battles and die young.

13) For the toughest decisions, use your head ... and your gut!

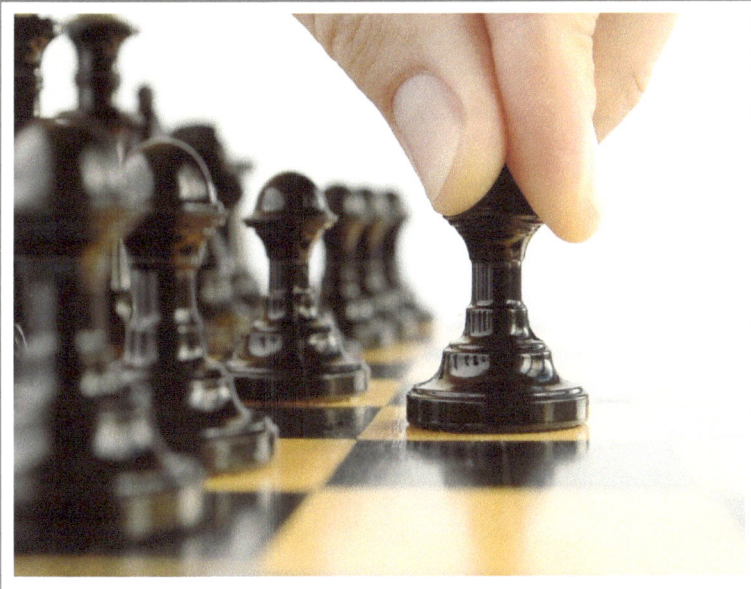

It's easy to get stuck when we're faced with tough decisions which carry a high risk factor, or when we're simply spoilt for choice. Situations which started off as low-key now become urgent as we struggle to move one way or the other and the pressure only seems to make our inertia worse. It's during these times that decisiveness is key to clearing the blockage and steering us clear from the impact-sapping habit of procrastination.

Some medical research suggests that our actions are directed not only by the brain, but also by the heart, often referred to as gut instinct. The brain plays an important role in weighing up the variables, the analytics, the conditionals, logical reasoning and pros and cons of a certain decision, asking key questions:

"How high are the stakes?"

"How much time do I have in order to make this decision?"

"What's in it for me?"

"What are the disadvantages?"

"How could this go wrong?"

"Is there a hidden agenda?"

"Is this something I can genuinely influence?"

As important as these angles are for making a considered decision, the sheer volume of information can trap us into over-thinking and avoiding the decision. Our gut however, operates at a deeper and more instinctive level and can indicate the right or wrong decision almost immediately. It's less concerned with the variables and more concerned with the right thing to do. When you act against your gut instinct, even if your mind can rationalise what you're doing, you'll still feel a sense of foreboding or unease about your actions because your gut is in disagreement.

Our best choices come when there's harmony between what our brain recommends and what our gut instinct confirms. If you want to become more decisive so that you achieve more, listen to the voices of your mind and your gut.

13) For the toughest decisions, use your head ... and your gut!

14) If you're struggling to focus and can't find inspiration, change your scenery, relax, and the inspiration will find you.

My daughters used to live with their mum in Dorset and every other Friday, I drove down the M5 from where I lived in Birmingham, to pick them up from school and return to my house for the weekend. It was a 3 hour drive each way. Because I hate being late and because the M5 is regularly at a standstill, I set out to arrive in Dorset for 12:00 to ensure I was never late. This usually left me with a 3-hour window of time before school ended for the day. I wanted to make good use of the time so I found a quiet pub nearby and started taking work with me to do while I waited. I discovered two things in the process:

1) The quality of my work there was noticeably better than anything I was doing elsewhere.

2) The most challenging aspects of my work were quickly resolved because once I was settled in the pub with my pot of tea (no beer; I was driving), my ideas flowed.

These fortnightly Friday sessions were uniquely productive and it got me thinking. What was it about that pub that had such an effect on the quality (and the quantity) of my work? It had less to do with the tea and everything to do with the impact of the environment on my ability to think.

There was no wifi in the pub, which meant no internet or email disturbance even if I'd wanted it.

The signal for my phone was lousy in the pub so no phone calls, no texts and still no internet!

The pub was quiet and obviously not the most popular establishment in town, which meant few distractions or noise.

My hands were free so I could immediately write my thoughts on paper or type them onto my laptop.

It was a different work setting. I only visited the pub each fortnight so it always felt relatively fresh as a space.

I had a specific 3-hour slot. This gave me plenty of time to settle, without the pressure that if my ideas were slow in coming, my time would soon be up.

I was positive and relaxed and always in a good frame of mind because I knew I was about to see my daughters who I greatly missed.

This is not a commercial for English country pubs. It's just that if you're struggling to make headway on a task which requires creative thinking, go easy on yourself (or your team), take a break and if you can, change your physical space (temporarily).

It could be a pub, or a cafe or a park bench, the point is to eliminate as many disturbances as possible, whilst finding a 'happy' space which helps you relax so the creative juices can get flowing. I've never quite grasped the inflexibility of some organisations who demand innovative thinking from their workforce on the one hand and yet maintain such rigid structures, that finding a peaceful space to think is almost impossible, (particularly if accessing such a space might take people out of the office!)

If you want to make a greater impact on your work, identify your own physical thinking space so you can:

Create a constant flow of ideas ... good ideas and lots of them.

Avoid getting stuck on the complex problems, something which drains your time and energy and also your confidence.

14) If you're struggling to focus and can't find inspiration, change your scenery, relax, and the inspiration will find you.

15) Productive people raise their game on significant things and lower their standards on trivial things.

After a bruising day at work, followed by the journey home, squeezed into your train carriages or parked up on the motorway, who wants the responsibility of putting a meal on the table or clearing the dishes afterwards? And then …

▶ What about the peeling paint in the bathroom? You said you'd see to it last week.

▶ Have you remembered that you've promised to pick Katie up from her friend's house?

▶ You'll need to get some fresh milk for tomorrow's breakfast. We're already running low.

It's easy to feel overwhelmed by the demands of every-day life and lose sight of what we really want to achieve. Many of us procrastinate on what we know we should do whilst pouring our energies into things which deliver little impact on what really matters. But amidst our demands and conflicting priorities, it's genuinely possible to achieve more without adding yet more things to an already long list of jobs to be done.

Of course, most of us want to live in a perfect house with a great garden. Most of us also covet the thought of a well paid job which we enjoy and which leaves us plenty of quality time for family and hobbies. But for many of us, this isn't real life and we simply burden ourselves with yet more stress if we are forever striving to get there.

If you want to be more effective at home, first, examine what you really want to achieve. In other words, take time to identify the things in your life, which would provoke an all-consuming euphoria in your heart were they to happen. Then consider the things which would cause you an unbearable level of distress if they happened. For most people, when they consider both angles, what really matters are the quality of their relationships and health rather than the state of their houses or their achievements at work.

Second, once you're clear on what really matters to you, clarify what action you're going to take to make things happen. The less important things on your list can always wait because quite simply, they're not as important as your key priorities and if you ever get round to achieving them, it's a bonus.

For example:

I keep my kitchen spotless (with the help of my wife and daughters) and it's like something out of an ideal show-home although the rest of the house definitely doesn't match it. We only iron what must be ironed (school uniforms and work shirts) and, during the week when our children have countless activities, we try to keep our home-cooked meals as simple as possible. As parents, we've made these decisions because we believe that quality time together, contributes towards one of our top priorities; the development of a deep, lasting and evolving connection with our children. We understand that because we're both working parents, we need to let go of certain housekeeping standards and expectations in order to achieve this priority.

It's too easy to fall into the trap of comparing ourselves with our neighbours and concluding that their lot in life is better than ours. But envy, comparison and wishful thinking all take our attention away from how and when we're going to make our mark on the things we value.

To stay focussed on the things which really matter to you:

Delight in what you do get done.

Stay calm about what you still have to do.

Be clear about what's important to you and pour your energies into achieving these things.

Stay clear of regrets, they'll only undermine your future impact.

15) Productive people raise their game on significant things and lower their standards on trivial things.

16) If you want to reduce your worries, act on those you can influence, ignore the ones you can't.

Does this insight seem out of place in this section?

Don't you think that material about handling worries fits better in the chapter on resilience?

Such material may fit well in the chapter on resilience, but the ability to keep your worries in check also has a direct impact on how productive you are.

It's been argued that 95% of the things we worry about never happen. On the one hand, it's comforting to know that most of our fears will never come to pass but on the other hand, they can still play on our minds, taking up precious nervous and mental energy which could be used elsewhere. Whether the 95% statistic is amateur guess work or an accurate figure, there can be little doubt that many of us waste a lot of time worrying.

There are a number of consequences which arise when we allow ourselves to become weighed down by worry. One of them is that the quality of our decision making becomes impaired because our thoughts have a massive impact on how we feel, our feelings then impact on how we behave, which finally shapes the decisions we choose to make. A simple example is this: if you're in love, you'll know what it is to think highly and to feel deeply about the person you love, and naturally these thoughts and feelings lead to all sorts of practical expressions of your love; it's love-in-action ... thoughts - feelings - behaviours - choices. Sadly of course, the reverse is also true: malicious thoughts and feelings too often provoke destructive action; which causes misery for all concerned.

It follows then, that if we're fretting about our worries, we're choosing to start a negative journey which leads from our thoughts to our feelings, then to our behaviour, ending finally with our actions. The outcome is that we become less effective, delivering little positive impact in our world and often alienating ourselves from the people who mean most to us.

For example:

I used to worry that my daughters would get so tired of the long journey from Dorset to Birmingham on Friday and the return on Sunday that they would decide to end this fortnightly ordeal by motorway - in other words, they would choose to stop seeing me at weekends. The weight of the worry made me feel stressed, which made me grumpier with my friends, colleagues and also my daughters when I saw them. The worry gave me sleepless nights, which made me tired, so I became even grumpier and more worried - another vicious circle!

In response to this negative spiral, I developed my own personal worry scale to help me think clearly and I've used it regularly ever since:

Outside my influence   Within my influence

1   2   3   4   5   6   7   8   9   10

Using the scale, I plotted this particular worry as a '5' because some of the outcome was completely beyond my ability to influence. My daughters clearly have their own personalities and at that time they made some of their own decisions. I was also mindful of the fact that you can't control what someone else will do, particularly when you only see them once per fortnight and, furthermore, I certainly could not control what my ex-wife, (and my daughters' primary carer) might do. So this was not a worry where I had a high degree of control but that said, there were still some practical things I could do to influence the outcome. I therefore concluded that '5' was about right and set out to identify five actions I could take.

I bought flat panel DVD screens for the headrests of my car so that my daughters could watch a movie as we cruised along the motorway. This would help alleviate their boredom on the journey.

I subscribed to 'Lovefilm' so that I had a constant supply of new movies for them to watch.

I prepared a picnic for both journeys with some treats to make their snacks interesting rather than predictable. I've generally found that well-fed children tend to be happier than hungry children!

I found a warm and welcoming pub at a half-way point in the journey and come rain or shine, we always stopped there to use their services, stretch our legs and buy crisps on both legs of the journey.

I resolved to get to bed earlier in the nights before their weekends to ensure I was on my best form (not tired and irritable) and the best dad I could be for them.

With five separate action points identified and implemented, I became peaceful that I was doing everything within my power to offset the likelihood of this worry from ever happening, so guess what? I quit worrying about it!

This very simple 'worry scale' works well because it helps you to examine each worry logically, calculating what level of control you might have so you can decide what level of action you're able to take.

These days, I only worry about things I know I can influence and I take specific action to make that influence practical. And when something is beyond me to affect, I refuse to give it the time-of-day.

16) If you want to reduce your worries, act on those you can influence, ignore the ones you can't.

BE INFLUENTIAL

17) Wise negotiators view objections as windows rather than stumbling blocks: when objections are handled with care, they teach something new about the people involved and the situation itself.

In my 'leadership' and 'sales' workshops, I ask people to draw what comes immediately to mind when they hear the word, "objection". It comes as no surprise that in nearly every case, they draw something negative like a stop sign, a sad face or a brick wall.

Unfortunately, this is a common perception of objections and it explains why so many people are defensive when others disagree with them. It's only natural that we seek agreement from others because whether we're prepared to admit it or not, we all feel a sense of personal affirmation when those around us support who we are, what we say and what we do.

The likelihood is that we've all been in that place when our point of view has been challenged and we've become aware of a rush of blood as we sense we've been put on the spot. It's not a nice feeling and more often than not, rather than embrace the objection in order to learn something new, we close down any chance of progress through our language (body or verbal) and everyone goes home dissatisfied.

If we're serious about enhancing our impact, the loss of potential self development from such a negative approach to objections, not to mention the break down in rapport with those around us, are both too serious to ignore.

If someone objects to what you're saying, or doing, or proposing; whether it's your children, your colleagues, your client or your boss; grab the objection as a learning opportunity with genuine potential for all sorts of fresh insights.

See windows, not walls, sad faces or stop signs.

Soften your body language and facial expressions so you appear open and thoughtful, something which encourages the other person to allow you to take a closer look through the window.

Ask open questions to encourage others to explain their point of view. One of my favourite questions for responding to objections is to calmly ask, "what makes you say that?" Then take time to listen to the answers, which means stay focussed on the other person, keep your mouth closed and overcome the urge to interrupt with "yes, BUT"!

Thank the other person for their opinion, whether you appreciate what's been said or not. Then it's up to you to decide:

▶ Is this genuinely a helpful yet painful learning point?

▶ Does this 'feedback' need to be discarded because it was blatantly issued in order to damage me and/or has a hidden agenda?

Nowadays, when I'm on the receiving end of an objection or a refusal, my ability to see it as a window helps me to override my instinctive defensiveness with a more open approach. I regularly remind myself that if I can handle the situation with calm, the other person may allow me to step closer and I'll be the one to benefit from this particular window of opportunity. By contrast, if I react too quickly, the curtains/blinds will be firmly shut and with it, all hope of mutual learning.

17) Wise negotiators view objections as windows rather than stumbling blocks: when objections are handled with care, they teach something new about the people involved and the situation itself.

18) If people follow your lead because they fear you, your influence will be short-term until fear turns to contempt; it always does.

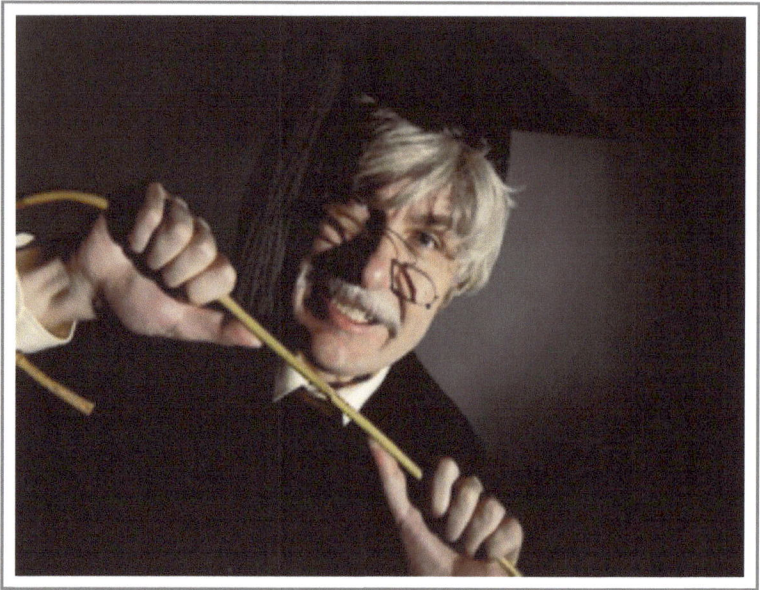

Darren was a typical 'old-school' manager. Unfortunately, he was also my boss for two difficult years. His approach was to bully people into accepting targets which he and they knew were unreachable, and subsequently pull them to pieces when the inevitable happened. A recent graduate, I wasn't too high on confidence at the time and it didn't take long before I was reduced to an anxious, corner-cutting and inward-looking plodder.

Intimidation was Darren's preferred method for extracting the best out of people. The result was that within two years, I was the sixth most senior person in an office of 30 people. Why did they all leave? Darren was unsurprisingly a common factor!

There is a major problem with the use of 'fear' (some might call it 'pressure') to motivate the people we lead. Sure, it can seem to work in the short-term and for a simple reason: no one wants to be on the receiving end of a blatant kicking so, when we're duly intimidated, we respond initially by pulling out extra stops and increase our productivity. Spurred on by the illusion that the fear factor is therefore delivering the goods, such leaders make the fatal mistake of staying with it - a serious leadership blooper!

It's not just old-school business managers who get it wrong. Some parents resort to their own brand of parental bullying which they believe will discipline their children into unflinching obedience. Of course, they wouldn't dream of calling it 'intimidation' - after all, how else do you impose your authority and ensure that your children know their place? But that's what it is.

Most of us want to leave a lasting impact. We'd like to think we're favourably remembered by the organisation we left four years ago and hope our ex-colleagues still think we did a great job. We hope our children and grand-children will be unanimous in thinking that we were devoted, loving, fun to be with and wise. None of us would be comfortable to accept that once we've gone, we're quickly forgotten, or worse, that our legacy stirs up ill feeling. But a lasting and positive impact requires the exercise of great influence and such influence is not possible if we rule through fear. It does however become possible when people follow our lead through their own free will because they trust our judgement and see us as both credible and caring.

If you stick with fear, time passes, and the raised voice, the demoralizing criticism, the threat of physical punishment (whether or not it's ever inflicted) and all other expressions of disapproval suffer a conspicuous loss of impact. Bit-by-bit, fear is turning into contempt. This is a more frequent feature of family life than we may care to admit. Children become teenagers - young adults - and, somewhere in the process, if parents have taken the 'fear is discipline' approach, children suffer a serious loss of respect for the very people they ought to be able to hold in highest regard. Such parents can no longer expect to influence the continuing development of their sons and daughters.

Something similar happens at work. Eventually people tire of being afraid and one of two things tends to happen: either fear turns into ill-concealed contempt which usually surfaces as rebellious anger or total apathy, or people leave and join a different organisation, bitter about the way they were treated by their former employer.

To summarise: line managers who use intimidation to do their job:

▶ Lose the support of the people they lead.

▶ Undermine staff creativity because people who are afraid, switch to survival mode and do only as much as it takes to survive; they don't risk any new initiative … hardly a healthy climate for the innovative culture which is so important for businesses operating in today's environment.

Whether it's children bullied by intimidating parents, a nation under dictatorial rule, a team afraid of its boss; the fear may work today but not tomorrow. It will turn into contempt. It's not a question of 'if', only of 'when'.

18) If people follow your lead because they fear you, your influence will be short-term until fear turns to contempt; it always does.

19) 'Bossy' delegation creates resentful robots - 'coaching' delegation creates productive performers (without the resentment).

"I've told them how to do it a thousand times but they still keep asking me how to do it!"

"Unless I tell them what to do, things either don't get done or they don't get done properly."

Most of us will have said something like this before because at some point, most of us will find ourselves in a leadership role either at home or work and we'll experience the frustration of our instructions being seemingly ignored. When things go wrong or they simply don't happen, it's easy to blame other people for not listening properly or for losing sight of what you originally set out for them to do. The best leaders however, recognise, that if their team struggles to deliver the task they left for them, there's a good chance it's linked to the leader and the way it was delegated.

In his best-selling book, 'The 7 habits of highly effective people', Steven Covey identifies two contrasting forms of delegation: 'Gofer' and 'Stewardship'. I prefer to call them 'bossy' and 'coaching'.

Bossy delegation involves telling someone everything: what the job is, when it must be done and step-by-step how it must be done. The emphasis is on the delegator giving orders and the delegates following those orders to the letter. People who are subjected to this form of delegation have virtually no input into the process because it's assumed that the (bossy) delegator knows best.

People-in-charge typically resort to bossy delegation:

▶ When they're under pressure and need to delegate quickly. They assume it's better to fire out a list of immediate instructions than to provoke deeper thought around the task.

▶ When they need the ego boost of assuming a superior position (they wouldn't admit to this, and probably wouldn't recognise it in themselves).

The biggest issue with this kind of delegation is that it delivers poor long-term results. It may seem to work well at first because it's an instant process, but that single advantage is far outweighed by the numerous disadvantages:

People only remember a few things at a time: The more information you give in one go, the less likely people are to remember what you've said (however brainy they may be). Even when they appear to be listening to you, they're unlikely to be retaining what you say. And when the same issue reoccurs, you'll have to repeat everything you've already said … again and again.

Bossy delegation causes resentment: Most people will only accept so much bossing around. Whoever the delegator is and whatever the delegator has achieved, bossy delegation should be the exception, not the rule.

Bossy delegation doesn't develop people: If you boss your colleagues, you stop them thinking for themselves and they become dependent on you for solving their problems. In other words, your form of delegation achieves virtually nothing for their long-term team development and you, as the bossy delegator, lose the benefit of their un-tapped potential.

By contrast, coaching delegation is focused on outcome rather than method. Coaching delegators trust their team's ability and accept that whilst trust involves risk, it also inspires performance and encourages ownership. In coaching delegation, the delegators work with staff to identify hazards, minimise risks and achieve goals; people own what they have helped to create.

Coaching delegation: May appear time consuming: Because of the risks in allowing people to find their own way in how they complete the task, a greater amount of time will initially be required to ensure they've explored the parameters of the task, the resources available, potential hazards and level of autonomy you're prepared to give.

Offers effective training: Coaching delegators help their teams to be creative in every aspect of their work. They're not just focussed on the completion of each task as they arise, they're also passionate about equipping each person to handle even more complex tasks as their skills develop. This has to be good news; a win-win situation for all concerned.

Encourages two-way learning: Coaching delegators know that they learn as much as they teach. It's easy to stick with what's worked well in the past but when we delegate real responsibility, we encourage new ways of thinking which may well challenge us to do things differently. It's good for humility and everyone benefits.

If you want a team of resentful robots, you have only to plaster the people you lead with a mass of detailed instructions before repeating yourself again and again when they forget what you've said. As a consequence, you're left with robots who learn virtually nothing new; you find yourself under even greater pressure because they're utterly dependent on you; they resent your approach, something which ultimately limits your ability to influence how they behave. Your robots may decide not to terminate you but your bossy delegation will limit their potential impact ... and yours too!

If you want to produce a team of competent performers, switch to a coaching model. Take time to ask those probing questions which empower people to think for themselves. Coaching delegation will ultimately produce more time for you because empowered and affirmed team members are more effective.

When I delegate at home or at work, I try to adhere to my 6 X 'R' model in order to deliver a coaching approach whilst minimising the element of risk.

1) Reality Check

    2) Result

        3) Risk inventory

            4) Resources

                5) Ramifications

                    6) Relationships

Reality check: Ensure the job you're delegating matches the capabilities, or at least the potential capabilities of the people to whom you delegate.

Results: Create a clear, mutual understanding of the intended goal, focussing on what is wanted as a result rather than how the result will be achieved.

Risk Inventory: Help your team to identify the potential hazards of the task you're delegating by asking exploratory questions. Create a joint set of parameters to which you and they can work.

Resources: Ensure they know what resources are available to them, including the level of support you intend to give.

Ramifications: Emphasize the difference between a job that is well done and one that is not. This is less about putting them under pressure and more about helping them to see the value of their work, which will help them produce better results.

Relationships: Focus not only on the successful completion of the task but also on the development of your relationship with the team. Good delegation provides a unique opportunity for you to develop rapport but you have to foster that relationship from the first bell to the final whistle. If things go wrong (it does happen): stay calm, avoid finger-pointing and ask "how can we avoid this happening again?"

19) 'Bossy' delegation creates resentful robots - 'coaching' delegation creates productive performers (without the resentment).

20) You get in life what you're prepared to accept so work out what you're prepared to accept, because that's what you'll get.

Derek was a former colleague and his son, Robert, (who was 13 at the time) was a major challenge to his dad. Robert was often missing from school and in trouble with the police. Many a time he'd arrive at our offices to ask his dad for money. Looking back, this must have been painfully embarrassing for Derek not least because the course of their 'conversation' was always the same:

Robert: "Dad I need money."

Derek: "Sorry son, I gave you money yesterday."

Robert: "It's all gone and I need some today."

Derek: "Well that's tough. I've got no money on me."

Robert: "Dad, I need money now. Come on."

Derek: "I'm not giving you any money and that's that."

Robert: "Dad I need money. Give me some money."

Derek: (exasperated silence)

Robert: "Dad?"

Derek: "Here's ten pounds son."

Robert knew his dad's "no" wouldn't last (and so did Derek). He'd get the money sooner or later; it was just a question of how long it would take him to break his dad's resistance.

Does Derek deliver any meaningful impact in Robert's life? (other than being an available cash point)

Sadly, Derek's ability to influence Robert's behaviour had become limited because he'd lost sight of what he was prepared to accept in life. His lack of personal boundaries simply encouraged his son to take advantage of his weakness and Robert wasn't the only one to do so. Clients, colleagues, friends; it was known that Derek was a weak touch so people treated him accordingly.

Successful influencers know what they're prepared to tolerate from other people and understand that their personal 'bottom line' will determine much of what they experience in life. In other words, they recognise that their sanity, enjoyment and success in life are closely linked to their ability to communicate and adhere to their personal boundaries. Without clear boundaries, it's almost inevitable that you'll:

Be a regular victim of deliberate distractions (you know what's happening but you've chosen to become powerless to do anything about it).

Regularly over promise and under deliver because you've allowed yourself to be pulled in all directions. As the pressure mounts, you lose the ability to think clearly and you resort to making promises which everyone knows you won't keep. Your hope is that the promises will buy you time, hopefully popularity as well. But the truth is that people lose faith in you, which seriously limits your ability to win their support when the chips are really down - no influence - no impact!

Take on too much. You feel overwhelmed yet still unable to say "no". As your work piles up and your promises multiply, you know you're in trouble (again). This is a classic route for likely workaholics, when you feel bound to stretch your hours to the point where the damage you suffer (and maybe inflict) is long-term for your relationships and your health.

Become manipulated by the loud voices in your team. You've shown that you're not tough enough to stick to your word and the stronger characters have pounced on it! Now, you find yourself tolerating too much from them although you may well hang on to some authority over the 'easier' people. This blatant inconsistency destroys everyone's respect for you. You've ceased to be the leader in anything more than name - no influence - no impact!

Whether we're leaders or team players, if we want to be successful within our roles whilst maintaining good emotional health, it's up to each of us to decide our own boundaries based on our values and our standards. The next step is to communicate them clearly and stick to them, even when under pressure. Consider the following questions and apply them to the different parts of your life:

▶ What behaviour would you accept from other people?

▶ What things are you prepared to compromise on and why?

▶ Which of your boundaries are immovable 'brick wall' boundaries and which are flexible, 'temporary fencing' boundaries?

▶ Are your boundaries logical, reasonable and defendable?

20) You get in life what you're prepared to accept so work out what you're prepared to accept, because that's what you'll get.

21) We're inspired when we have something to believe in and something to hope for.

It's hardly rocket science to work out that there's a chasm in potential between people who are highly motivated and people who are not. For any leader, coach or parent seeking to make an impact in the lives of those they lead, they must first understand the basics of how to inspire people to be at their best.

Some leaders and managers still prefer the traditional 'stick and carrot' approach. In essence, criticise and bully if people under-perform (stick); reward with praise and bonus if they do well ('carrot'). (Clearly those who favour this approach see their team members as horses or mules, which isn't the best starting point for inspirational leadership!)

Daniel Pinks, best selling author and business coach, argues against this practice. He believes that when people are in high-pressure situations, it's detrimental to their ability to think creatively if their principal motivation is the prospect of a reward for getting it right, rather than a job well done for its own sake. For Pinks, the reward culture can lead to a mistaken focus which actually produces errors of judgment and therefore inferior performance. Instead, he favours an approach which allows people the autonomy to take responsibility for themselves, so they give of their best because they want to achieve the best possible results: it's called job satisfaction!

I believe that the key to motivating other people involves a vital four-letter word ... HOPE!

Sure, I can be motivated if I want to better myself or if I'm simply excited because I think I could produce something special. Equally, I may be just as motivated if I'm trying to avoid the painful consequences of not performing well. But, at a deeper level than this, my motivation is rooted in my self-belief and my self-belief is rooted in how much I dare to hope.

If you've lost hope before; at work, home, sport, hobby; even an oppressed nation suffering the tyranny of a ruthless dictator, it's part of that loss of hope to conclude that there's nothing you can do to influence the situation and things will never change. Almost inevitably, apathy sets in, as does a despairing, all-pervasive sense of 'what's the point?' and hopelessness takes over. It's at this stage that people become disengaged from their purpose and as a result, their productivity dips. Regardless of how much they're pushed, encouraged, threatened or bribed, when people lose hope, they also lose their creativity, resilience, enthusiasm and belief. No amount of 'stick and carrot' will bring these things back because if there's no hope, you're simply flogging a dead horse!

Our resolve for action depends on the strength of our hope. Once we start to hope that things could be different, we then begin to believe that they might be and see things that we couldn't see before. We suddenly realise that we do still have an element of control over the situations we face and our mind moves to considering how we can influence some of our desired outcomes. Finally, this new conviction motivates us to take action, either because we want to do something brilliant or because we want to prevent further pain and limit the damage.

You may be a leader at work or a parent at home but if you're looking to inspire other people to 'want' to take action and achieve something great, you must be consistent in communicating a clear and credible message of hope.

**21) We're inspired when we have something to believe
in and something to hope for.**

22) If you expect people to follow your instructions, be sure to avoid the word "don't".

Let's be honest, we've all been there and we've all done it:

"Don't step in the road, you could get hurt."

"Don't play on the fence, it might break."

"Don't send it like that, she's our best customer."

When we give an instruction, we hope people will do what we say, even if we have our doubts that they will. We may be parents warning our children of approaching danger or business leaders trying to raise the bar in our organization: when we request something from our children or our colleagues, we're looking for them to listen to what we say, to act on it and to remember for next time.

The problem with "don't" is simple: it doesn't matter how many times you give your instruction, if you begin with a "don't", whoever's on the receiving end will focus almost exclusively on the very thing you're telling them not to do rather than on what you actually want them to do!

In other words, "Don't go there because ..." almost certainly means that people end up thinking about 'going there'. Instructions which start with a "don't" seem to create their own automatic 'brain-bypass' and you'll need to repeat yourself endlessly before your real intention gets through.

Unfortunately, the more you bark out the same old orders, the more time you waste, the more frustrated you become and the more you confirm your unwanted reputation as an old nag. The problem is, as we all know, that old nags exercise very little influence and, without influence, you can forget about 'impact'.

For example:

Imagine a sweltering, hot day, the sweat's pouring off you, you're gasping for a drink but you're miles from anywhere. So I say to you, "don't think about a cold, orange, ice-lolly; the juicy, sweetness of the oranges, the ice refreshing you, cooling you down; just don't think about it." All you can do now, whether you like it or not, is to think only about the lolly, completely forgetting that you were told, "don't". It's the same for adults as it is for children, and it happens regardless of the situation.

If you do need to give instructions:

1) Keep them positive and be specific about what you want to happen. Take my word for it, eliminating "don't" can be harder than it sounds. It requires practice and takes time.

"Don't step in the road, you could get hurt."

"Walk on the pavement because it's safer."

"Don't play on the fence, it might break."

"Get off the fence and leave it alone. It's flimsy and might break."

"Don't send it like that, she's our best customer."

"This document needs more work on it. It looks messy and I've already spotted a few errors in the text."

2) Coach rather than command (particularly in situations where there's no immediate danger.) Ask questions to stimulate thought about the situation. Good questions keep people engaged and help them take ownership of their actions:

"Don't step in the road, you could get hurt."

"Why's the pavement a better place to walk than the road?"

"Don't play on the fence, it might break."

"What could happen if you keep playing on the fence?"

"Don't send it like that, she's our best customer."

"If you send the document like this, what do you think our client will think?"

22) If you expect people to follow your instructions, be sure to avoid the word "don't".

23) If your 'apology' begins "I'm sorry if ..." / "I'm sorry but ..." you communicate irritation not regret.

I once heard it said on a youth impact coaching course that young people won't care what you think until they think you care. This is surely also true for adults and I'd go one step further by suggesting that other people won't care what you think until they know you care. Sure, if you're an expert on your subject, people will listen to you at one level. But, at a deeper level, they'll only open up and fully engage with you if they've decided that it's safe to do so, because they 'know' you care.

As leaders, exercising a specific leadership role, there are many things we can do to reveal the level of our care for the people for whom we're responsible. Some of the more obvious include:

1) Taking a genuine interest in the people we lead: What makes them tick? What are their challenges and how can we support them? What are their skills and how can we most value them?

2) Supporting not blaming when things get tough: As per the insights in the first chapter on resilience, identify positive learning points when your team hits problems - avoid finger-pointing.

3) Being ready to apologise when we've made a mistake: Perhaps we went too far in our rebuke of a colleague? Maybe the team's poor performance had as much to do with how we led the task rather than with the team's inadequacies?

An apology is not a sign of weakness, it's a sign of great strength. When leaders 'know' how to apologise and do so freely, it has a powerful effect on their connection with the team and sets the tone that within this group of people, it's ok to be open about your mistakes.

For example:

'Despicable Me' is a great family movie but unfortunately it doesn't bring back the best of memories for my wife. We went as a family to the cinema with great expectations but towards the end of the film, she realised that her knee length jumper and jeans had become damp. Unfortunately, she'd been sitting on a seat, which I imagine a small child (in need of potty-training) had been using during the earlier showing of the film!

When we spoke with the cinema manager, we were polite in our approach but she was immediately defensive. Her first response was to insist it wasn't her or her staff's fault (we never suggested it was) before putting us in the position where we began to regret ever having mentioned it. She also uttered those fatal words, "I'm sorry if you feel we've let you down ..." which in this context, basically meant:

"I'm annoyed that you've approached me with this. I don't care about your stupid jumper and frankly it's not my fault or problem. I wish I could end this conversation quickly, but you're a customer so I'll give you a half-hearted apology and hope you go away."

In the end, her attitude strengthened our determination to stand our ground and she finally gave up by grudgingly offering us two free cinema tickets. Of course, the wet seat was not her fault personally, but we were dissatisfied customers with a legitimate grievance and it was her responsibility to put things right. Any self-respecting manager would be looking for a gesture to ensure that the 'damp seat incident' was not the defining feature of our visit to 'her' cinema.

When things go wrong on your watch, you have an opportunity quite as much as a problem: to show your care in such a way that you build new levels of trust with each person involved. We all respond to those who make a generous effort on our behalf, particularly if they're humble and are trying to put something right. So, if you want to exercise real influence, be deliberately positive when problems arise and, when you do apologise, think about **W.A.R**!

Why:

We'll want to know 'why'/'how' things went wrong because that's the way we find out whether or not it's likely to happen again. By exploring the 'why', we make it clear that we're taking the situation seriously and we're not just looking to skate over the problems with a hasty but meaningless "sorry". In these situations, apologies need a 'why' as well as a 'sorry'.

Apology:

The apology needs to be genuine and sincere, which means, NEVER say, "I'm sorry if you feel we've let you down." Apologies should ALWAYS be stated clearly, specifically and without 'if' or 'but'. (Also take care with your use of the word 'that' so you're not tempted to say, "I'm sorry that you feel I've upset you" which clearly means, "I don't think I've upset you and the problem is really with you, not me.")

Using the example of the cinema manager, what she should have said was:

"I'm sorry you've been let down. There's not much time between each movie so we don't check every seat and generally we just about have time do a quick clear up of the obvious mess. That said, it's our responsibility so we'll ..."

Resolution:

Human relationships are generally not unconditional. Therefore to make the most of an unfortunate event, you need to do something to resolve the situation. It's not enough to ask the victim what they would like you to do - it's up to you to make a heartening offer, using your initiative, creativity and generosity.

"I'm sorry you've been let down. There's not much time between each movie so we can't check every seat and generally we just about have time do a quick clear up of the obvious mess. That said, it's our responsibility so I'd be pleased to offer you some free tickets to another movie of your choice. Please accept my sincerest apology."

When we're strong enough to offer genuine apologies, we demonstrate a willingness to be vulnerable, something which indicates to others that we have integrity because we've nothing to hide. If people believe we have integrity, they'll allow us to have influence, and when we have influence, we can make a BIG impact.

23) If your 'apology' begins "I'm sorry if ..." / "I'm sorry but ..." you communicate irritation not regret.

24) Effective leaders ask themselves, "what will it take for the people I lead to see me as credible?"

Pippa Middleton, sister of the Duchess of Cambridge, Kate Middleton, took some serious stick in 2013 over her column in the Waitrose kitchen magazine, (Pippa's Friday Night Feasts). To be fair to her critics, her foodie ideas weren't exactly remarkable but what really riled them was a perceived lack of credentials for the job in hand; she was trading on her name rather than her expertise.

There are many of us who could commiserate with Pippa's need to step out of her sister's shadow and few of us could blame her for grasping the opportunity to write a column for such a prestigious organisation. But what both Pippa Middleton and Waitrose failed to grasp, was that people will not allow themselves to be influenced by someone who they think lacks credibility.

For Pippa's column to have been successful, her writing would have had to be out of this world, breaking boundaries and exceptional. It would also have helped her cause if she'd had some serious catering experience or Cordon Bleu training to support her suggestions. What's true for Pippa Middleton is also true for you and me as we consider our leadership roles. In order to make a huge and positive impact as a leader, we must first understand the 'criteria for credibility' within each unique group of people we lead.

Let's imagine: you've just been appointed to lead a demoralised team. Your predecessor was a ruthless control-freak who's left behind a legacy of non-existent self-belief and conspicuous resentment of authority. In this case, because of the team's previous experiences, a leader's 'criteria for credibility' is likely to include a constant demonstration of positivity, gentleness and a consultative approach to decision making.

On the other hand, a team which has enjoyed consistent success under the guidance of an experienced leader, would be more likely to place a higher value on a new leader with a similar track record of success, and perhaps a lower value on a leader who had a gentle or positive spirit but whose track record was less impressive. The 'criteria for credibility' in other words, are the steps which each leader must take in order to secure the trust of the people they lead. Ask yourself:

▶ What will it take for me to get my team to a point where they trust my judgement? (even in the tougher times)

▶ What leadership approach will work best with this unique group of people?

▶ How does their history shape their expectations of their leaders and what does this mean for me?

When you're faced with a new team of people, or you feel you've lost the edge with the team you currently lead, consider the question of credibility very carefully. Credibility dictates whether or not people will follow you freely and passionately because when you're seen as credible, people accept your judgement more easily and believe in you for who you are, what you do and what you say. Credibility can be easily lost and won but the reasons for losing and winning it will vary from team to team because no one group of people is ever exactly the same.

24) Effective leaders ask themselves, "what will it take for the people I lead to see me as credible?"

WHAT INSPIRED 'THE IMPACT CODE'?

Everyone wants to make an impact on something and for most people, there are a number of aspects in life where this desire runs so deep that, if they were unable to make it, the road to personal crisis would be a painfully quick journey.

Why do so many people suffer a mid-life crisis?

Why do so many people work towards the 'freedom' of retirement, only to lose their purpose shortly after it happens?

Why do so many of us become 'de-railed' when an aspect of life is not going the way we want it to go?

Quite simply, we flounder when we think we're not making the impact we expected to make and before we know it, we then start to believe a crushing lie, that we're no longer useful. On the other hand, when we know we're delivering an impact and sense we're exercising a positive influence, we grow in self-confidence, glowing from the inside-out.

I'm passionate about helping people to 'glow' for the long-term, something which is dependent on how resilient, productive and influential they can become. It's therefore been my privilege to have shared a range of strategies and insights through 'The Impact Code', so that you're fully equipped to make your mark.

The first insight, (resilient people see their problems as temporary and their strengths to overcome them as permanent) was inspired by the brilliant sports psychologist and friend, Mark Sheasby. His unique, I.M.P.R.E.S.S. coaching model, has been extensively used in the sporting and business world.

ABOUT THE AUTHOR

Andrew Pain:

I've lived and worked in France, Mexico, El Salvador and am now settled in Birmingham, UK. I work extensively as an accredited coach and business trainer with large blue-chip clients, public sector organisations, small to mid-sized businesses, the third sector, unemployed young people and a variety of individuals.

I'm happily married with two superb daughters aged 13 and 10. We also have a joyful and bouncy toddler, who's yet to discover the wonders of sleep but who regularly has his sisters and parents in fits of laughter! I enjoy attempting to play football (I'm no Lionel Messi), spending time with my family, and snowboarding when possible, which isn't often in Birmingham! Most people who meet me think I look far younger than I am (I'm 40). I take it as a compliment and my wife certainly doesn't complain about it (yet).

I'd be delighted to connect and interact with you personally on social media:

Follow me on twitter *twitter.com/andrewpain1974*

Connect with me on Linkedin *linkedin.com/in/andrewpain*

Connect with me on Facebook *facebook.com/ImpactLifeUK*

Check out my website *www.impactlife.co.uk*

Check out my blog *andrewpaincoaching.blogspot.co.uk*

Choose to make an awesome impact in your world ... or don't ... it's up to you!

www.ingramcontent.com/pod-product-compliance
Lightning Source LLC
Chambersburg PA
CBHW041710200326
41518CB00001B/145